MW01204529

Children of the World

Cuba

For a free color catalog describing Gareth Stevens' list of high-quality children's books, call 1-800-341-3569 (USA) or 1-800-461-9120 (Canada).

For their help in the preparation of *Children of the World: Cuba*, the writer and editor gratefully thank: Professor Michael Fleet, Marquette University, Milwaukee; Professor Howard Handelman, University of Wisconsin-Milwaukee; and Lillian Rodriguez Kalyanaraman.

Library of Congress Cataloging-in-Publication Data

Cummins, Ronald.
      Cuba / photography by Mercedes Lopez ; written by Ronnie Cummins.
         p. cm. — (Children of the world)
      Summary: Presents the life of a twelve-year-old boy and his family in Cuba, describing his home and school activities and discussing the history, geography, ethnic composition, natural resources, sports and recreation, government, religion, and culture of his country.
      ISBN 0-8368-0219-5
      1. Cuba—Description and travel—1981- —Views—Juvenile literature. 2. Cuba—Social life and customs—Pictorial works—Juvenile literature. [1. Family life—Cuba. 2. Cuba.] I. Lopez, Mercedes, 1961- ill. II. Title. III. Series: Children of the world (Milwaukee, Wis.)
F1765.3.C86 1990   972.9106'4—dc20   89-43170

A Gareth Stevens Children's Books edition

Edited, designed, and produced by
Gareth Stevens Children's Books
1555 North RiverCenter Drive, Suite 201
Milwaukee, Wisconsin 53212, USA

Series editor: Valerie Weber
Editor: Amy Bauman
Research editor: Mary Jo Baertschy
Designer: Laurie Shock
Map design: Sheri Gibbs

Printed in the United States of America

   2 3 4 5 6 7 8 9 96 95 94 93 92 91

Children of the World

Cuba

Written by Ronnie Cummins
Photography by Mercedes Lopez

Gareth Stevens Children's Books
MILWAUKEE

. . . a note about *Children of the World*:

The children of the world live in fishing towns, Arctic regions, and urban centers, on islands and in mountain valleys, on sheep ranches and fruit farms. This series follows one child in each country through the pattern of his or her life. Candid photographs show the children with their families, at school, at play, and in their communities. The text describes the dreams of the children and, often through their own words, tells how they see themselves and their lives.

Each book also explores events that are unique to the country in which the child lives, including festivals, religious ceremonies, and national holidays. The *Children of the World* series does more than tell about foreign countries. It introduces the children of each country and shows readers what it is like to be a child in that country.

Children of the World includes the following published and soon-to-be-published titles:

Australia	El Salvador	Japan	Spain
Belize	England	Jordan	Sweden
Bhutan	Finland	Malaysia	Tanzania
Bolivia	France	Mexico	Thailand
Brazil	Greece	Nepal	Turkey
Burkina Faso	Guatemala	New Zealand	USSR
Burma (Myanmar)	Honduras	Nicaragua	Vietnam
Canada	Hong Kong	Panama	West Germany
China	Hungary	Philippines	Yugoslavia
Costa Rica	India	Poland	Zambia
Cuba	Indonesia	Singapore	
Czechoslovakia	Ireland	South Africa	
Egypt	Italy	South Korea	

. . . and about *Cuba*:

Twelve-year-old Alain lives in Havana, Cuba's capital city replete with historic buildings and a rich past. He practices hard at his fencing and harmonica and plays baseball, a favorite Cuban sport. Alain is fascinated by stories of distant countries and exciting times, and he listens eagerly to his father's tales of his world travels and his grandmother's accounts of her days as a guerrilla fighter during the Cuban revolution.

To enhance this book's value in libraries and classrooms, comprehensive reference sections include up-to-date data about Cuba's geography, demographics, currency, education, culture, industry, and natural resources. *Cuba* also features a bibliography, research topics, activity projects, and discussions of such subjects as Havana, the country's history, political system, ethnic and religious composition, and language.

The living conditions and experiences of children in Cuba vary tremendously according to economic, environmental, and ethnic circumstances. The reference sections help bring to life for young readers the diversity and richness of the culture and heritage of Cuba. Of particular interest are discussions of the changes in Cuba since the revolution and its relationship with the United States and the USSR.

CONTENTS

Above: Alain Alfonso Lamar (lower left) is seen with (clockwise, from left) his aunt Xandra (pronounced *Sandra*); a family friend; his aunt Martha; his mother, Xonia (pronounced *Sonia*); his brother, Alberto; and his grandmother, Carlota. Like most Cubans, Alain's name has three parts. His first name is followed by his father's family name and then his mother's family name. Opposite page: Alain and Alberto greet their father, who is also named Alberto, at Havana Harbor. Behind them is the oil tanker *18th of April*, the ship on which Alberto works. ▶

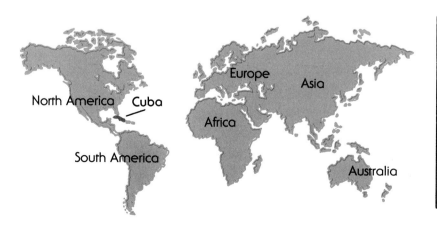

LIVING IN CUBA:
Alain, a Boy from Havana

Twelve-year-old Alain Alfonso Lamar thinks Havana, Cuba, is an exciting place to call home. There, Alain lives in an apartment near the city's center, with his father, mother, brother, aunts, and grandmother. Alain's father, Alberto Alfonso Fernandez, works on an oil tanker and is often at sea for months. Alain misses his father when he is gone and excitedly awaits the ship's return to Havana Harbor.

Between 1956 and 1959, a young man named Fidel Castro Ruz led a rebel army in a revolution against Fulgencio Batista y Zaldivar, an unpopular dictator. After the revolution, the government nationalized, or took over, all private business. Thus, the government owns the oil tanker on which Alberto works, and he works for the government. Since the revolution, almost everyone in Cuba does.

Alain's Neighborhood

Alain read that Spanish explorers founded Havana in 1515. The city, with a population of over 2 million, presents a blend of old and new. A building over one hundred years old, for example, often stands next to a modern structure. Alain's family lives in an apartment building built in the 1950s, but their neighborhood is much older. The area is called Vedado, which means "forbidden." It earned that name when the Spaniards, who occupied Cuba from 1515 to 1898, forbade slaves or poor people to live in or even walk in this part of the city.

From his home, Alain can walk to parks, museums, and movie theaters. The Caribbean Sea is just a short distance away, too. Alain often wanders along the walkway, called the Malecón, that runs beside it. From there, he watches the big ships sail into Havana Harbor, always hoping that his father is on the next one.

Above: Alain looks over the upcoming movies listed on a billboard outside of Cinema Yara. This theater is one of many movie theaters in his neighborhood.
Opposite page: From the rooftop of the family's apartment building, Alain can look out over a section of Havana. Havana's mix of old and new, as seen here, gives the city its character. ▶

People constantly mill about the streets near Alain's home. Many of them are tourists staying in the large hotels nearby. Alain welcomes the chance to speak with people from other countries. His father's stories of distant places have excited his curiosity about life in other countries. Alain intends to visit many of these places when he is old enough. In the meantime, he studies about them. In high school, he will study both the English and Russian languages. The government stresses studying these languages because of their value to relations between Cuba and other countries. Alain thinks these languages will also help him in his travels.

A bus crowds an already busy street near Alain's home. Buses are the main form of public transportation in Havana.

The balcony at the end of the sixth-floor hallway is one of Alain's favorite getaway spots. From here, he has another grand view of his neighborhood and some of the nearby hotels.

Alain's family lives in a five-room apartment on the apartment building's sixth floor. Alain says the best thing about their building is the balcony at the end of the hallway on each floor. From the balcony on his floor, Alain can look out over the entire neighborhood. If he leans way out over the railing, he can even see the ocean.

11

The sprawling city of Havana, as seen from the top of the Havana Libre Hotel in the center of the city. Some of the central city's stately old buildings stand in the foreground, while newer, more modern buildings rise in the background.

A Typical Day in Havana

Alain usually wakes up at about 7:00 a.m. He makes his bed, straightens his room, and dresses for school without being told. His mother, Xonia, who wakes at about the same time, has chores to tend to before work, so Alain often cooks his own breakfast to help out. If he has time, he even cooks for her. Today, he makes a breakfast of fried eggs and buttered toast. The egg yolks turn out perfectly this morning; he hopes his mother notices.

Because he has a little extra time after breakfast today, Alain pulls out his stamp collection. He wants to look again at the new stamps that his father has sent him. Alberto's work takes him all around the world. As he travels, he often picks up stamps for Alain's collection. The newest stamps, which arrived in the mail just yesterday, come from Mongolia — a country in Asia near China.

Left: With a steady hand, Alain prepares to flip the egg he is cooking for his breakfast.
Opposite, inset: Alain proudly shows the book that holds his stamp collection. ▶
Opposite: A page from Alain's collection. These stamps — some of his favorites — depict some of Cuba's popular sports. They were issued in honor of the 1980 Summer Olympic Games in Moscow. ▶

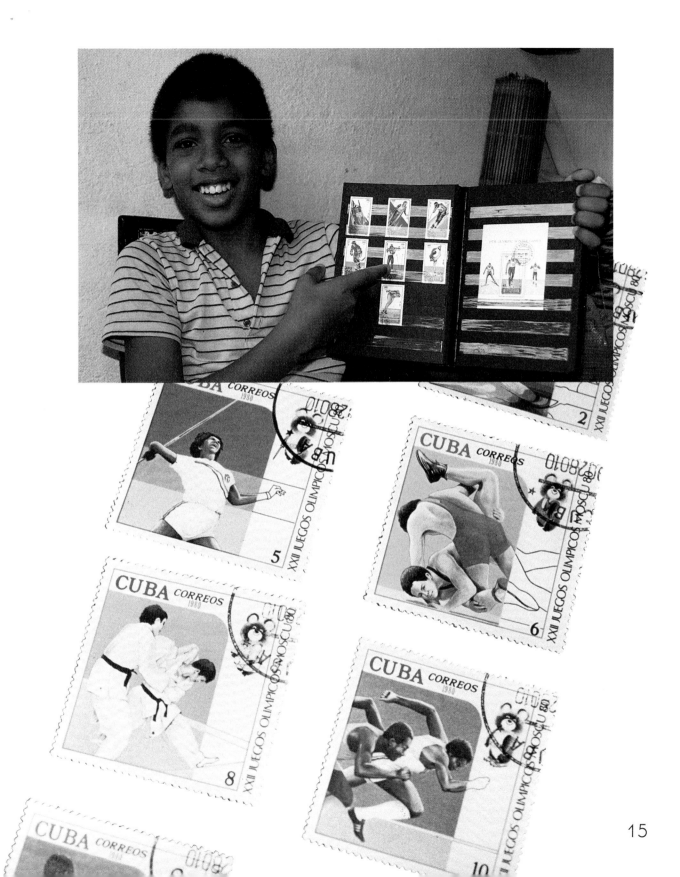

15

As he often does before school, Alain walks to the neighborhood market with his aunt and his mother to buy a few items. The government owns the corner market, which carries basic foods such as grains, dairy products, vegetables, and canned goods. If Alain's family wants to buy fresh fruit, meat, or fish, they must shop at a different neighborhood store.

The government subsidizes the food at the corner market — that is, the government pays part of the cost. As Alberto has explained to Alain, this system keeps prices low on basic foods so that even poor families can afford to eat properly. As part of this system, Alain's family, like every other Cuban family, has a food ration card that determines how much of each kind of food they can buy at the low, subsidized price. To buy more than the amount shown on the card, they must pay a higher price. As Xonia and Alain's aunt Xandra pick out the items they need, he checks the card to see if they will be allowed to buy them.

◀ Opposite page: A crowd gathers in the neighborhood store. Although small, this store carries many basic foods, and it is just down the street from the apartment.
Below: Alain pays for this morning's items, which include milk. When buying milk, Cubans bring their own milk bottles to the store to be refilled.

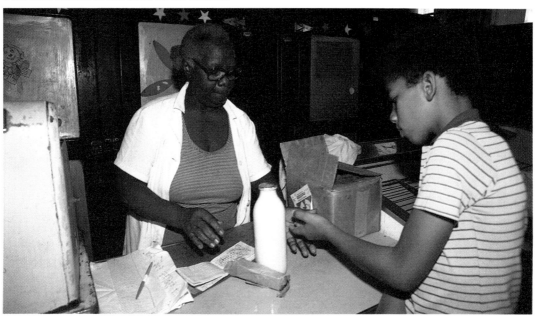

Looking at the clock, Alain sees that he must hurry to school. While he attends school, everyone else in the family has a job to go to. Xonia, an accountant, has a job in a health care center. His aunt Xandra is a construction engineer, while his aunt Martha works for a film and video production company. Alain's brother, Alberto, who is 20, has a job as an electrician's assistant in Varadero, a nearby beach resort. Alberto lives in Varadero during the week but comes home on the weekends.

Alain's grandmother, Carlota, has just recently retired. Looking at his grandmother, Alain thinks that few people would imagine that she is 56 or that she fought in the Cuban revolution. But Carlota has told many stories of the time when, as a young mother, she joined the rebel fighters in the mountains of Cuba. Her collection of medals — awarded to her for bravery in battle — proves that the stories are true.

Dressed in his school uniform, Alain is ready for school. On his way out the door, he stops to say good-bye to his mother.

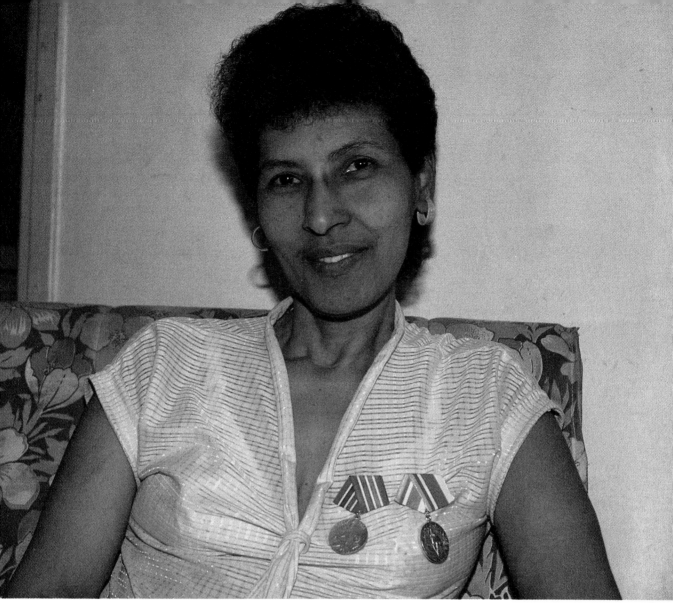

Carlota displays the medals she earned fighting for the revolution. One is for the organizational work she did in the city. The other is for the year and a half that she spent fighting in the mountains.

Alain's School

Alain walks to school each day since his school is only three blocks away. Now a seventh-grader, he attends Ruben Martinez Villena School in Vedado. The school, named for a Cuban revolutionary hero, was once an enormous private mansion. Now, it houses grades seven through twelve.

In Cuba, taxes pay for education. By law, children between the ages of 6 and 18 must attend classes, which run from September through June. Most students wear uniforms, which the government provides. The colors of the uniforms vary according to which grade the student is in. Wearing the yellow and white uniform of the upper grades this year, Alain feels very grown-up. When he was in the lower grades, he wore a red and white uniform. Like many students, Alain wears a red *pañuelo*, or bandanna, around his neck.

Below: Alain often walks to school with his best friend, Tony, who lives on a lower floor of Alain's apartment building.
Opposite page: Alain stops to talk with a friend at the gate of the mansion-turned-school. ▶

Cuban schools stress science and math, but the teachers spend much time teaching literature, social sciences, and the arts. With his wild imagination, Alain does well in literature, but even math and science come easy to him. Before graduating, all students are required to perform public service as part of their studies. Often the assignment has students cleaning up the environment, planting trees, or helping out during harvest time. Alain hopes that his assignment will have something to do with science.

Today, Alain practices *esgrima*, which is Spanish for "fencing." Many of his friends also fence, so Alain can always find a practice partner. Since fencing requires much skill and can be dangerous, Alain and the other fencers wear padded uniforms and face masks to avoid injuries. Alain hopes to participate in fencing tournaments and maybe even become a member of Cuba's national fencing team when he is older.

◀ Opposite page: Alain stands with classmates in the school yard after classes. Because it is near the end of the year, everyone seems very relaxed. When final exams are through, the students will take part in an end-of-the-year custom — signing each other's shirts and blouses.
Below: With several adults living in the same house, Alain never has trouble finding someone who is willing to help him with his homework.

Alain Tours Old Havana

The old section of Havana, with its three ancient castles, fascinates Alain. When walking through Habana Vieja, or "Old Havana," Alain wonders what it must have been like in the 16th and 17th centuries, when pirates and soldiers fought fierce battles here.

The first castle Alain visits is the Castle of the Moors. The Spaniards built this castle between 1589 and 1630, after pirates attacked the old city. This castle, which is surrounded by a wide moat, overlooks the city's channel and main harbor. In 1844, the people of Havana added a lighthouse to the castle. Alberto has told Alain that he can see the powerful light from about 19 miles (30 km) out at sea. After a long voyage, Alberto says he watches eagerly for the lighthouse beacon as his ship nears Havana Harbor.

Havana Harbor as seen from the Castle of the Moors, a castle built to protect the harbor and its city.

Alain strolls out toward the second castle, the Castle of the Point. The city officials have turned this low, sturdy fortress into a museum. Looking at the castle's thick stone walls and the old cannons out front, Alain imagines a fierce battle taking place. Then, spotting the monument to Máximo Gómez, a leader during Cuba's 1868 revolt for independence, Alain thinks about the many people who gave their lives for Havana and Cuba.

The third castle, the Castle of the Force, has the honor of being Cuba's oldest surviving building. From his history lessons, Alain knows that this castle was built in 1538 after another serious pirate attack on the city. He also knows that after the Spaniards built the first castles and forts, they went on to build the plaza, the cathedral, and the other main buildings of Old Havana. As Alain walks along the cobblestone streets, names, dates, and places important in Cuba's independence struggle fill his mind.

Alain and Xonia take their time exploring the castle's many rooms and exhibits. Here they stand before a Spanish rug that was made in the Canary Islands.

◀ Opposite page: Alain and Xonia make a second stop at the Castle of the Point. A museum has been built inside this castle, and today's exhibit includes artifacts and handicraft from Spain.

Alain and Xonia come upon Plaza de Las Armas, Havana's main plaza. This plaza has hosted many of the city's historical meetings, celebrations, and parades. A large ceiba tree grows in the plaza, marking the grave of Christopher Columbus. Not far from the tree, Alain sees the statue of Carlos Manuel de Céspedes, another leader in the 1868 revolt for independence.

The Municipal Palace, erected in 1776, stands near the plaza. The Spanish governors and presidents lived there until 1917. Today it serves as Havana's historical museum. Another building, called La Tinaja, houses a natural spring that the Spaniards discovered. Because it's hot today, people crowd inside La Tinaja for a drink of water. Alain admires the building's stone and tile work, as well as the restored houses, shops, restaurants, and hotels around it. Rather than fight the crowd at La Tinaja, Alain stops at a nearby café for a cool fruit drink.

◀ Opposite page: Alain and Xonia stop to rest beneath the ceiba tree in the middle of Plaza de Las Armas. Cuba's first Catholic Mass took place beneath this tree.
Below: Alain examines old church bells in front of the Municipal Palace. The bells came from the Havana Cathedral, which is also in Old Havana.

After a tough day at school, there's nothing like a trip to Coppelia Park. There, a cone in each hand is the rule.

The World's Largest Ice-Cream Parlor

After school, Alain and his friends often stop in Coppelia Park, which is just four blocks from Alain's apartment building. No matter when Alain stops, the park — often called the world's largest ice-cream parlor — overflows with people. People crowd the park's hundreds of tables and benches, eating every imaginable flavor of ice cream and sherbet. Even more people stand, waiting for a seat.

Alain stands in line to buy ice-cream tickets for everyone. He can't decide whether to buy an ice-cream cone or a *helado ensalada* ("ice-cream salad") — a combination plate of several ice-cream flavors. Alain is surprised to learn that many North Americans would consider this a lot of ice cream. In Cuba, adults and children often eat more than one cone at a time. After finishing their ice cream, Alain and his friends relax among the trees, talking of the flavors they'll try next time.

30

Alain can keep up with the rest when it comes to eating ice cream.

Alain spots an old Nash Rambler from the 1950s behind a neighboring building.

Havana's Cars

From the apartment balcony, Alain watches automobiles moving below him.   Many cars that he sees are US-made cars from before 1960. After the Cuban revolution, the United States prohibited trade with Cuba, so new US cars are rare. The Cubans have kept the old cars running, and many of them remain in almost perfect condition. From his perch, Alain can identify the model and year of almost every car passing below him.

Cuba now trades mainly with the Soviet Union and Eastern Europe. So most newer cars in Cuba are Soviet Ladas, which look something like Italian Fiats. New Ladas cost 5,000 Cuban *pesos* (about $6,600), which is well over the average Cuban family's annual income. Like most Cubans, Alain's family uses public transportation, which is cheap, reliable, and convenient for traveling around Havana or across the island.

Right: Havana's streets are filled with US cars from the 1940s and 1950s.
Below: Alain imagines taking a ride in the sidecar of this flashy red motorcycle. Motorcycles are a popular form of transportation.

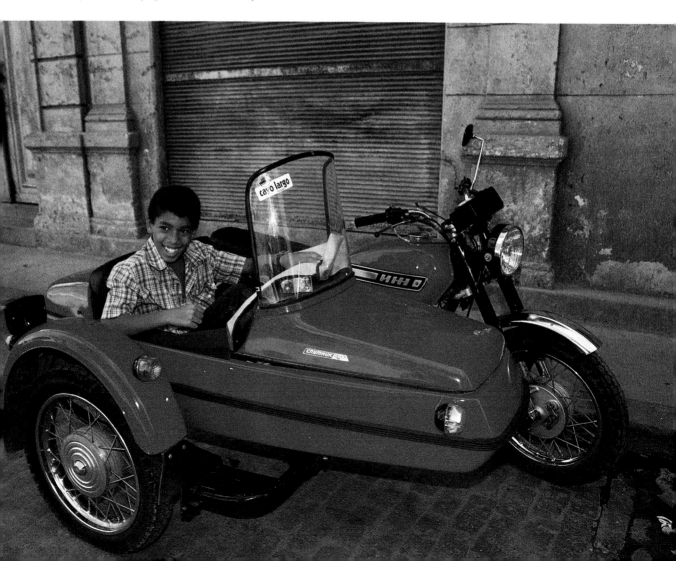

In his bedroom, Alain amuses himself with his harmonica.

The Weekend at Last — Time to Relax!

Alain relaxes on weekends. If his mother doesn't need help, he sleeps late. When he wakes up, he watches television, reads the newspaper, or listens to the stereo. Often, he plays along with the music on his harmonica. Sometimes, when she's especially tired, Xonia asks him to practice in his bedroom or on the balcony.

Alain looks forward to the weekends, knowing that Alberto will come home from Varadero. The brothers usually spend part of the weekend just talking together. For a little privacy, they climb to the roof terrace, where, in addition to a great view of the neighborhood, they can usually find a breeze.

The midday sun beats down on Alain and Alberto as they sit on the apartment building's rooftop. Alain looks forward to this time alone with his older brother.

Weekends also give Alain time to work on his stamp collection. Since Carlota retired, she has joined Alain in this pastime, and he gladly accepts her help. His collection contains mostly commemorative stamps, which mark special occasions. Some of his favorites depict the Olympic Games. Above all others, though, Alain prizes the stamps from faraway countries he hopes to visit one day, such as the Soviet Union, Vietnam, and China. He can't wait until he is old enough to travel.

Like nearly everyone else in Cuba, Alain loves watching, playing, or listening to baseball. Local games are played all around him daily, but occasionally he even sees games in the Havana sports center. The weekend gives him a lot of time for his sports. Besides baseball, Alain fills his free time practicing his fencing, lifting weights, and playing basketball and soccer.

Alain calls Tony to arrange this afternoon's baseball game.

Opposite page: Perhaps because he is the youngest member of a large family, Alain has learned to amuse himself. Between his friends, and his many interests, Alain is never bored. On some days, all it takes is a handful of marbles, and Alain can entertain himself for hours. ▶

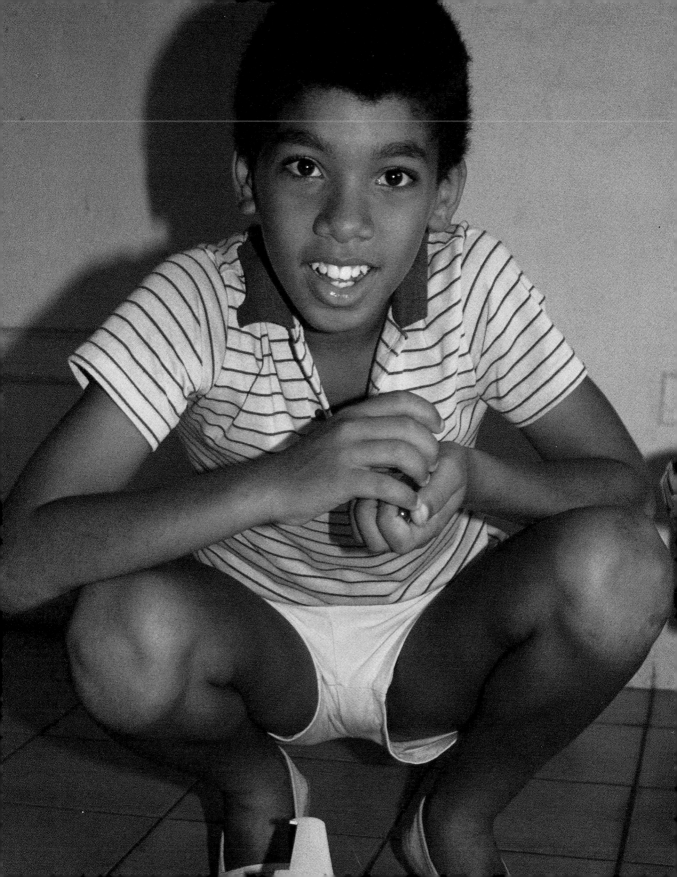

Above: *Bienvenidos al Parque Lenin* —
"Welcome to Lenin Park." The sign at the
entrance to Parque Lenin greets visitors. This
amusement, cultural, and educational park is
located about 6 miles (10 km) from the center
of Havana.

Right: Just inside the park stands an enormous
monument honoring Vladimir Lenin. No matter
how often he sees it, Alain is always awed by
the size of the sculpture. A tribute to Lenin,
written by Fidel Castro, has been engraved into
the monument's base.

A Day in the Park

Parque Lenin, Havana's largest and most popular park, is named after Vladimir Lenin, the Soviet revolutionary leader. Located at the city's edge, the park includes a botanical garden, museums, arts and crafts workshops, trails for horseback riding, and an amusement park. It covers 1,655 acres (670 ha) of land, but a coal-powered locomotive that runs throughout the park makes travel easy.

Today, as Alain and his aunt Xandra enter the park, they stop to look at the huge sculpture of Lenin. Then they walk to a French teahouse for an iced drink. Near the teahouse, the park train passes them, carrying many passengers. Most public trains now run on diesel fuel, so Alain is fascinated by the old coal-burner. The train engineer toots the whistle as they pass. Everyone waves.

The park's coal-burning train passes Alain and Xandra. This time, it is filled with park employees. Alain calls hello, and the men clown for the camera.

Alain hurries Xandra on to the open-air theater, where plays and concerts are held. Climbing onto the stage, Alain imagines performing in front of a large audience. From the stage, he spots a group of school friends. They chase each other until Xandra calls Alain to get something to eat. They eat at the open-air market, where Alain orders pizza with lots of cheese and hot sauce.

After lunch, they're off to the amusement park, where Alain rides every ride. The Ferris wheel and the roller coaster, called the "Russian Mountain," he rides a few times. He tells Xandra that the roller coaster is exciting because it sometimes feels as if the roller-coaster car is going to shoot off its rails and fly into space. Alain also wants to test his skill at the shooting gallery. Usually he can hit the bull's eye, but today his aim is off. After one more ride on the roller coaster, it's time to go home.

Top: After a morning in the park, Alain has worked up a monstrous appetite. It takes a whole lot of pizza, tamales, and drinks to quiet his growling stomach.
Above: The park is a favorite spot for class trips. Here, a group of schoolgirls take turns getting a drink of water from a waterspout.

Alain rides the Ferris wheel, called "Star Viewer," several times. Because the park is quiet today, he gets one of the cars all to himself.

Above: "Ready to dance?" Alain asks, putting an album by Sergio Mendes on the stereo.
Left: The family's collection of albums includes musicians who sing in both English and Spanish.

The Family Plays Together

Music is a constant part of Alain's life. At home, someone is always digging through the family's records, looking for a favorite artist to play on the stereo. Alain often listens to Sergio Mendes, who sings in both Spanish and English, or the Cuban folksinger Sylvia Rodriguez. He also has the records of such singers from the United States as Lionel Richie and Ruben Blades. Harmonica in hand, Alain dreams of becoming a famous musician.

Everyone in Alain's family loves to dance. When they're all at home, they often move the furniture aside, put on a record, and dance. The Vedado neighborhood often hosts street dances, and young and old alike come to listen to live bands and dance. Someone's having a street dance this afternoon; Alain can hear the music from the apartment. When his mother and aunts come home from work, Alain knows that they will want to join the street dancers.

When the music starts, Xonia grabs Alain's hand and gets him to dance with her. Although Alain loves to dance, he is shy about it.

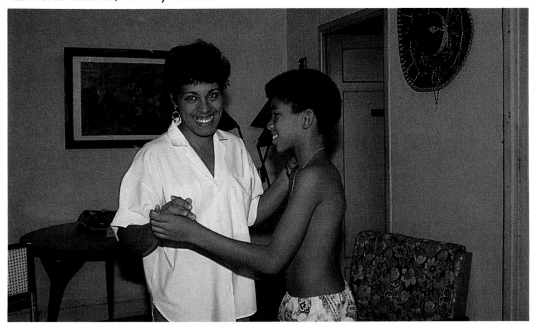

Everyone in Alain's family is always willing to go to a movie. Havana has 166 movie theaters that show films from all over the world, so the family has many movies from which to choose. Alain's neighborhood alone has about a dozen movie theaters. Whenever a Walt Disney film plays nearby, Alain and his friend Tony go to see it.

Recently, Xonia took Alain to a poster and craft exhibit in Old Havana. At the exhibit, Alain spent a lot of time looking at traditional African-style wood-carvings, while his mother discovered the miniature dolls in their colorful costumes. They were both interested in the collection of Cuban political posters. The posters, which were collected over the last 30 years, make statements about current Cuban and world problems.

At the poster and craft exhibit, Xonia spends much time looking at the miniature dolls. The dolls wear festive costumes from different parts of Cuba.

Alain does not mind looking at the dolls, but the wooden carvings fascinate him much more. Many of the carvings show the influence of African culture on Cuba.

An Afternoon at the Beach

On weekend afternoons, Alain often hops on a city bus for an afternoon at the beach. Xandra doesn't have to work, so she and Alain go together. The beach, which is only 9 miles (15 km) from Havana, is one of Cuba's beautiful white sand beaches. Cool, dark blue Caribbean waves roll on the sand, and Alain can barely wait until the bus comes to a stop before he takes off running for the water.

Alain splashes in the waves, close to shore. He knows how to swim, but he also knows it's best not to swim too far from shore, where the current can be very strong. He meets some young men and talks them into taking him for a ride on their catamaran. As the boat cuts quickly through the water, Alain breathes in the salty air and feels the ocean breezes racing against him. His father has often said that there is nothing quite like the ocean. Alain agrees.

Alain and his family often visit Santa Maria Beach, where he swims, plays in the waves, and builds sand castles. Today, he is lucky enough to catch a ride on a catamaran.

47

FOR YOUR INFORMATION: Cuba

Official Name: República de Cuba
(ray-POOH-blee-kah day KOO-bah)
Republic of Cuba

Capital: Havana

History

Cuba's Early History

Natives belonging to three major tribes dominated early Cuba. These three tribes were the Siboneyes, the Taínos, and the Guanajatabeyes. When Christopher Columbus landed in Cuba on October 27, 1492, an estimated 100,000 natives were living on the island. The island seemed so large that Columbus believed he had discovered a new continent. Because Columbus and his men also thought that they had landed in Asia, near India, they called the natives that they met "Indians."

Havana Cathedral is one of the old buildings that still stands in the city. Roman Catholic priests had the cathedral built in 1704.

48

When Columbus arrived, these natives already had a well-organized social structure. They lived by gathering, hunting, fishing, and farming with tools made of seashells, stone, and wood. They had never seen a metal spear, a sword, or a horse, and according to Columbus, they were a friendly, peaceful people. He was equally impressed by the land, describing it as "the most beautiful land my eyes have ever seen." Although it was not rich with the gold and silver he had hoped to find, Columbus claimed the territory for Spain.

About four years later, Diego Velázquez founded Cuba's first Spanish colony, Baracoa, on the island's eastern end. By 1515, Velázquez had established seven towns, including Havana, the future capital. Needing laborers to help in establishing their towns, the Spaniards tried to force the local people to work for them. Some of the Indians surrendered, but others, led by an Indian chief named Hatuey, fought the invaders. Hatuey and his warriors fought fiercely, but lacking weapons and armor, they were no match for the Spaniards. Eventually, the Spaniards captured and killed Hatuey. His death marked the end of the Indians' rebellion.

The Era of Slavery and Spanish Colonialism

In their colonies, the conquistadores established a system known as the *encomienda*. Under this system, the Indians were resettled on huge plantations, or encomiendas, where they served the Spanish colonists. The colonists claimed that the encomienda was a good system because it civilized the Indians. From the natives' viewpoint, it was nothing more than slavery.

Spanish domination proved harsh. Thousands of Indians died of starvation and overwork. Others died from contagious diseases that the conquistadores brought from Europe. By 1526, so many Indians had died that the Spaniards began to import blacks captured in Africa to work as slaves in Cuba. In the 1550s, although the Spaniards had conquered Cuba less than 50 years earlier, they had reduced a once-thriving native population to only 5,000 people. By 1600, the entire Indian population had been wiped out.

At about the same time, the Spanish colonists introduced sugarcane to Cuba, and this crop soon became the island's main crop. As the sugar industry grew, however, the plantation owners needed more labor. Between 1600 and 1886, hundreds of thousands of Africans were forcibly brought to Cuba to work on the sugarcane, tobacco, and fruit plantations. By working these slaves hard, the plantation owners grew rich. Before long, the colony of Cuba was known as the "Jewel in the Spanish Crown."

Cuba's location between the Old World and the New World eventually brought it importance as a trade center for goods traveling between Spain and the New

World. Its rich soil, warm climate, and large slave population soon made it Spain's most valuable Caribbean colony. But other countries also saw the colony's worth, and Cuba was often attacked by Spain's rivals, England, France, and Holland. In 1762, during the Seven Years' War, the English managed to capture the island. They returned it to Spain a year later in exchange for the territory of Florida.

The Spanish did bring limited social and economic change to Cuba. In the early colonial years, in addition to sugarcane, the Spanish encouraged such industries as cattle, timber, and tobacco. They also built churches, schools, and other urban buildings. As early as 1592, they built an aqueduct to carry water for drinking and irrigation. In 1728, the University of Havana opened, and Spanish culture and arts flourished, though usually only among the rich.

In the nineteenth century, many of Spain's New World colonies demanded independence. Eventually, Spain granted independence to most of its Latin American colonies, but because Cuba had become so profitable, Spain fought to keep it. As the Cubans began developing a sense of themselves as a nation — one abused by the Spaniards — a movement for independence began.

Until 1855, bloody uprisings plagued Cuba. The Spaniards reacted harshly to the rebellions but were unable to quash them. Black slaves, poor people, landowners, and intellectuals stood side by side in the revolts. Despite the movement's determination, the Spanish authorities refused even to discuss independence or to make needed reforms in the country's laws. Under Spanish law, for example, no Cuban could hold public office or establish a factory or a business. No Cuban had the right to bring a lawsuit against a Spaniard, and Cubans were not allowed to travel without military permission. Beyond this, black and white Cubans were forbidden to intermarry, and slavery existed until 1886. Under these conditions, mass rebellion was almost unavoidable.

In 1868, Cuban landowners, led by Carlos Manuel de Céspedes, declared Cuba's independence. Céspedes made the announcement, releasing his slaves and calling on all patriotic Cubans to overthrow the Spanish tyranny. Uprisings broke out all over the country, led by Cuban patriots such as Antonio Maceo, Máximo Gómez, and Calixto García. The 1868 uprising, known as the Ten Years' War, claimed 85,000 lives — including those of 35,000 Spaniards. It ended in 1878, when the Spaniards signed the Peace of Zanjón. By this treaty, the Spanish authorities promised to make needed reforms. But reforms, like independence, were slow in coming.

In 1895, another rebellion erupted, led by the Cuban poet José Martí. Today many Cubans consider Martí the "Father of the Nation." Although the Spaniards used their harshest methods to crush the rebels, the war lasted three years.

During the fighting, the Spanish army, commanded by General Valeriano Weyler, devastated the countryside and forced hundreds of thousands of people into concentration camps. North American and Latin American people alike were shocked and angered by "Butcher" Weyler's brutal tactics.

US Intervention

Even before hearing news of Weyler's tactics, the US government had been concerned about the war in Cuba. For one thing, the United States had long considered Spain an economic rival. Secondly, the United States didn't want a Spanish-ruled country in its "backyard," and Cuba was only 90 miles (145 km) to the south. In 1897, the United States asked Spain to end its brutality in Cuba.

On the night of February 15, 1898, the US battleship *Maine* — sent to protect US citizens living in Havana — was mysteriously blown up in Havana Harbor. Two months later, the United States declared war on Spain. US forces, including future president Theodore Roosevelt, invaded the island. After a few weeks of fighting, the Spaniards surrendered.

The United States and Spain signed the Treaty of Paris on December 10, 1898. Under this treaty, the United States was to control the former Spanish colonies of Cuba, Puerto Rico, Guam, and the Philippines during a transitional period. In Cuba, this transitional government lasted more than three years, until the Republic of Cuba was proclaimed on May 20, 1902. Even then, the United States government retained some control of Cuba by insisting that the Platt Amendment be included in the new Cuban constitution. This amendment basically allowed the United States to intervene in Cuban affairs.

Between 1902 and 1959, Cuba's government struggled for stability. Even strong leaders seemed unable to cope with the problems of the newly independent country. Sooner or later, most of Cuba's leaders became part of a cycle of corrupt politicians and military dictators. Cuban presidents Gerardo Machado and Fulgencio Batista were examples of this trend. Both men sought economic and social change for Cuba but eventually became known for corruption and the brutal persecution of opponents. For example, during Batista's second term, the government murdered 20,000 people and imprisoned and tortured thousands more. Batista was supported by the rich, who lived in royal splendor, while the masses struggled to survive. Finally, the Cuban people decided to overthrow the dictatorship, no matter what the cost.

Castro's Revolution and Present-Day Cuba

Between 1953 and 1959, Fidel Castro, then a young lawyer, and a following of students, urban workers, and farmers fought against the Batista dictatorship.

Castro began his political career in 1953 by leading a famous but unsuccessful assault against one of Batista's military barracks. After two years in prison for this attack, Castro was released and went into exile in Mexico. There he assembled a group of Cubans to return home and lead a revolution. Between 1956 and 1959, Castro's guerrilla army fought successfully against Batista's troops, eventually sparking major rebellions throughout the country.

The rebels finally defeated the government forces on January 1, 1959. Castro and his guerrilla army then took control, immediately making radical economic and political changes. The new government seized all foreign-owned lands and businesses, as well as all nonagricultural Cuban businesses. Even banks, public utilities, and foreign trade were taken over by the government. In addition, Castro's government changed the tax structure to penalize the rich and the middle classes in favor of the poor. Changes to improve health care and the educational system followed. Many people criticized the economic and political measures of the revolution because they seemed so radical. But the measures have raised the standard of living for the majority of Cubans.

At the start of the revolution, Castro tried to retain good relations with the United States. In time, the radical nature of Castro's government became clear to many people in the United States. For example, Cuba has established close ties with the Soviet Union, criticized US foreign policy, and encouraged revolutionaries throughout Latin America. As these events have unfolded, relations between the United States and Cuba have soured. Support from within Cuba has not been unanimous, either. Many Cubans, especially the upper and middle classes, which opposed the revolution, and even some people who supported it, were disappointed with the government Castro created. Hundreds of thousands of these people have left Cuba to live elsewhere.

Since the 1960s, the United States has forbidden trade with Cuba and restricted travel to the island by US citizens. The United States has also pressured its allies to stop trading with Cuba. This has greatly weakened the Cuban economy. Before 1959, Cuba's main source of trade and tourist revenue was the United States; Cuba now relies heavily on Soviet money. But economic and travel blockades were not the only US actions against Cuba. In 1961, a US-supported invasion force landed in Cuba and tried to overthrow the Cuban government. The invaders were quickly defeated by the Cuban army, and this invasion, known now as the Bay of Pigs invasion, was a failure.

Through the late 1960s and into the 1970s, Cuba's actions further alienated it not only from the United States, but also from much of Latin America. Not until the mid-1970s did Cuba express interest in improving its international relations. Since then, such relations have alternately warmed and cooled as many of Castro's policies continue to cause discontent both inside and outside Cuba. The number of people who have left Cuba since the revolution serves as a measure of this discontent. In 1980, Castro temporarily opened Cuba's borders, letting out anyone who wished to leave. At that time, over 125,000 Cubans left the country, bringing the total number of refugees to over one million

Government

Since the revolution of 1959, Castro and the Communist party have ruled Cuba. Under the 1976 constitution, the government divided the country into 14 provinces and 169 municipalities. It also allowed voting, which is done by secret ballot and is open to any Cuban 16 or older.

In popular elections, the people elect local leaders as well as those for their province. Many candidates are members of the Cuban Communist party — the only political party in the country. The municipal assemblies in turn elect leaders to the National Assembly of People's Power, which holds the supreme power in Cuba. The National Assembly has 499 members, called deputies, who serve five-year terms. From among its members, the National Assembly elects 31 people to form the Council of State, the highest governing body. As part of its duties, the assembly appoints people to the courts, called the Popular Tribunals, of its judicial branch. As is true of the other branches, the judicial branch has local, provincial, and national levels, with the People's Supreme Court as the highest judicial body.

The National Assembly also selects the president, who serves as both head of state and head of government. The president also heads the Council of Ministers. This council, whose members are appointed by the president and the National Assembly, handles many administrative duties. Fidel Castro has been the unquestioned leader of the government since 1959. Although his leadership was approved by the National Assembly in 1976, 1981, and 1986, his role is not challenged in national elections.

Climate

Cuba's location gives it a tropical climate with ample rainfall. The moist northeast trade winds blow across the island, cooling the land in the summers and keeping it warm and pleasant in the winter. Most of the island gets at least 45 inches (1,143 mm) of rain per year, which falls mostly between May and October. Occasionally in the winter, a cold air mass moving from the north brings near-freezing temperatures to the island's northeastern section. July is Cuba's warmest month, with an average temperature of 82°F (28°C). January is the coolest month, with an average temperature of 71°F (22°C). Winters are usually sunny and dry.

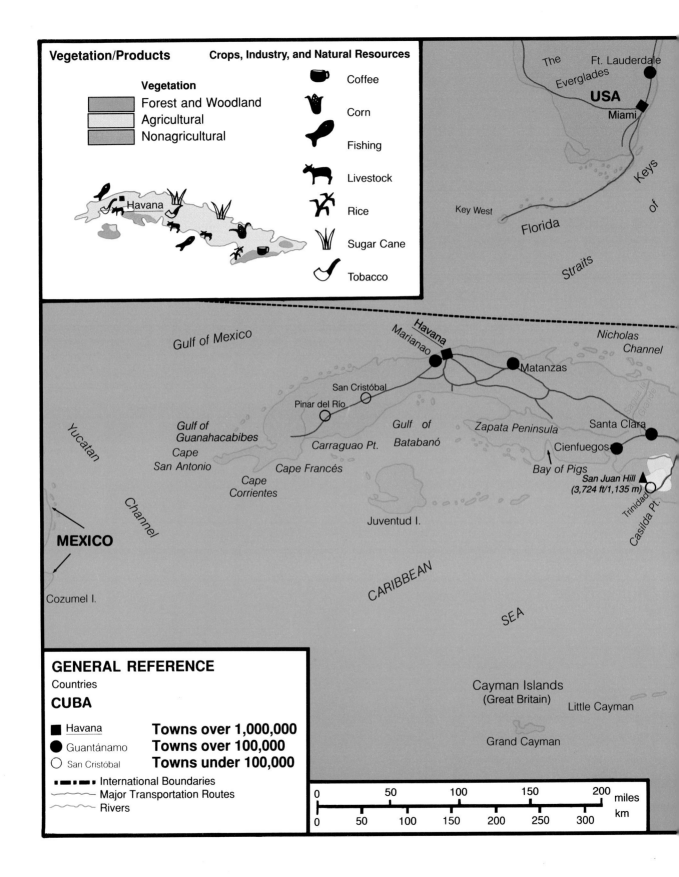

Vegetation/Products

Crops, Industry, and Natural Resources

Vegetation

Forest and Woodland
Agricultural
Nonagricultural

Coffee
Corn
Fishing
Livestock
Rice
Sugar Cane
Tobacco

Havana

The Everglades
Ft. Lauderdale
USA
Miami

Key West
Florida
Keys

Straits

Gulf of Mexico
Havana
Marianao
Nicholas Channel
Matanzas

San Cristóbal
Pinar del Río
Gulf of Guanahacabibes
Cape San Antonio
Carraguao Pt.
Cape Francés
Cape Corrientes
Gulf of Batabanó
Zapata Peninsula
Santa Clara
Cienfuegos
Bay of Pigs
San Juan Hill
(3,724 ft/1,135 m)
Trinidad
Casilda Pt.

Yucatan
Channel
MEXICO
Cozumel I.

Juventud I.

CARIBBEAN

SEA

Cayman Islands
(Great Britain)
Little Cayman

Grand Cayman

GENERAL REFERENCE

Countries
CUBA

■ Havana   **Towns over 1,000,000**
● Guantánamo   **Towns over 100,000**
○ San Cristóbal   **Towns under 100,000**
▪▪▪▪ International Boundaries
—— Major Transportation Routes
～～ Rivers

0	50	100	150	200	miles
0	50	100 150	200 250	300	km

CUBA — Political and Physical

Florida

Great Bahama Bank

Sanataren Channel

Nassau

Eleuthera I.

Andros I.

Cat I.

BAHAMAS

Tropic of Cancer

ATLANTIC

Crooked I.

Coco Cay

Old Bahama Channel

Romano Cay

Guajaba Cay

Arch. de Camagüey

Sabinal Cay

OCEAN

atibonico del Sur

Gulf of Ana Maria

Florida

Camagüey

C U B A

Puerto Padre

Cape Lucrecia

San Pedro

Nipe Bay

Jardines de la Reina

Holguín

Gulf of Guacanayabo

Bayamo

Sierra del Cristal

Guarico Pt.

Passage

Manzanillo

Palma Soriano

Guantánamo

Cape Maisí

Sierra Maestra

Turquino
6,561 ft/2,000 m

Gran Piedra
3,710 ft/1,131 m

Santiago de Cuba

Guantánamo Bay
(U.S. Navy Base)

Windward

Cape Cruz

HAITI

Montego Bay

JAMAICA

Port-au-Prince

Land

Cuba's 42,792 square miles (110,831 sq km) of land make it the largest island in the area of the Caribbean and Central America. It lies 90 miles (145 km) south of the United States. Other neighboring countries include Mexico, Jamaica, Haiti, and the Bahamas. Also known as the Cuban archipelago, Cuba is composed of one main island, a second sizable island called the Isle of Youth, or Juventud Isle, and about 4,000 smaller islands, keys, and islets. The main island, shaped like a crocodile, stretches about 760 miles (1,220 km) long and 120 miles (190 km) at its widest point. Numerous bays, peninsulas, and reefs give the country a total coastline of about 2,490 miles (4,000 km).

Although most of the country lies at sea level, several mountain areas rise in height from west to east. Elevations in the country range from sea level to 6,561 feet (2,000 m). At this highest elevation stands Pico Turquino, a mountain peak in the Sierra Maestra range on the eastern part of the island.

The action of rainfall on limestone formed about 80% of Cuba's soil. This process produced deep, fertile, and often bright red soil, in which more than 3,000 species of tropical fruits and flowers grow. Farming consumes 29% of the land area; pastures and meadows occupy 22%; forests cover 17.4%. To date, Cuba has set aside 10% of its land for parks and animal and nature preserves.

Natural Resources, Agriculture, and Industry

Cuba has a pleasant climate and vast areas of fertile land suitable for farming. These are among its finest natural resources. Its coastline offers excellent opportunities for its fishing industry, which is the sixth largest in Latin America. Cuba has also discovered significant mineral deposits. Deposits of nickel, the country's most plentiful mineral, account for 10% of the world's known nickel reserves. The country mines smaller amounts of iron ore, chromium, and copper, and continues to develop natural gas and coal reserves. Cuba produces a small amount of the petroleum it uses but imports 98% of its crude oil from the Soviet Union. Exploration for petroleum has uncovered significant deposits along Cuba's northern coast.

Sugarcane remains Cuba's leading crop. Spanish colonists introduced this plant to Cuba and found the country's soil and climate ideally suited to its growth. Sugar, then, is the country's primary export, followed closely by tobacco, coffee, and cocoa. Although the Soviet Union is now Cuba's major buyer, the United States held that position until the Cuban revolution. Since then, the Cuban government has invested heavily in meat, dairy, and citrus fruit production, but farmers continue to grow rice, potatoes, beans, and other vegetables.

The government owns 82% of the farmland, on which it operates state farms and cooperatives. Much of this land was originally part of the huge Spanish plantations, but the government seized these huge tracts of land after the revolution. In many cases, the government allowed small ranchers and family farmers to retain their land, and this group still holds 18% of Cuba's farmland.

In today's Cuba, the government decides which crops should be planted and to whom the produce will be sold. Because of shortages and export demand, the government also employs a system of rationing within the country. By this system, the government regulates how much of a certain rationed item each family may purchase. Rationing covers rice, bread, beans, sugar, coffee, meat, and other basic foodstuffs.

Cuba has a socialist economy, which means that the government, not individuals, owns most of the land and businesses. The government, rather than private owners, makes decisions relating to industry and the economy. Although Cuba has a mainly agricultural economy, the government has encouraged the development of certain other industries in recent years. The processing of minerals is one industry that Cuba is developing, and nickel is Cuba's second largest export. Other Cuban industries include medicines, textiles, chemicals, fertilizers, machinery, cement, gasoline, tires, cigarettes, cigars, shoes, crude steel, raw sugar, processed food, timber products, electric energy, and transportation equipment. Before the revolution, tourism was Cuba's third largest industry. Many tourists came from the United States until the US government halted travel to Cuba in the 1960s. Today, the United States government still restricts travel to Cuba, but Europeans, Canadians, and Latin Americans still travel to the island. With over 300,000 tourists visiting every year, tourism once again contributes a sizable amount of money to Cuba's economy.

Population and Ethnic Groups

Persons of Spanish or mixed Spanish and African descent compose the majority of Cuba's 10.5 million people. Whites make up about 66% of the population, blacks about 12%, and people of mixed race (a mixture of white and black) about 22%. Cuba's native Indian population was completely wiped out by 1600 as a result of the Spanish conquest.

Currently, over half of Cuba's people are under 30 years of age, and the population is growing by about 1% per year. About three-fourths of the people live in cities or towns, and the population density equals about 240 persons per square mile (93 persons per sq km). The United States has approximately 67 persons per square mile (26 persons per sq km), while Canada has only about 7 persons per square mile (3 people per sq km).

Education

The Cuban educational system has improved greatly since the revolution. The state pays for education at all levels, and often classroom study is combined with manual labor and public service. By law, children between the ages of 6 and 18 must attend school. Because of the government's emphasis on education, between 90% and 95% of the population can now read and write.

Education begins in preschools for children five years of age. Beyond that, children get 12 years of primary and secondary education. Recent statistics show that 98% of all primary-school-age children (ages 6 to 11) are attending classes. At the final level of education, students enter a university, technical school, or other specialized institution. In the 1980s, Cuba emphasized technical and scientific studies, especially medicine, engineering, economics, mathematics, and vocational instruction. The country has earned a reputation for its excellent medical training programs. Many students still attend one of Cuba's four universities, which have a combined enrollment of 85,000 students. About 55,000 of these students attend the University of Havana.

Religion

Although the Cuban government claims the country is an atheist state, Cuba still has many Christians within its borders. Of these Christians, the majority are Roman Catholics. In a 1980 poll, 48.7% of the people described themselves as nonreligious, 39.6% as Roman Catholics, 6.4% as atheists, 3.3% as Protestants, 1.6% as Afro-American spiritists, and 0.4% as holding other beliefs.

Culture and the Arts

The Cuban government actively promotes cultural activities within Cuba. The country has experienced a recent expansion of its museums, performance halls, movie theaters, art schools, and such industries as publishing and film and television production. Despite this growth, many of the arts have suffered from control by a government that expects artists and the arts to serve but not criticize the state. Writers have felt particularly restrained, and many have left the country.

Cuban culture, expressed through literature, visual arts, music, and dance, blends its Spanish and African heritage. This blend is perhaps most evident in music and dance, which continue to thrive in Cuba despite government influence. Afro-Cubanism, a movement celebrating this blend, took hold of the country at the beginning of the 20th century. The excitement of Afro-Cubanism has spilled beyond Cuba's borders, bringing the world such well-known dances as the rumba, the conga, and the tango.

Sports and Recreation

The Cuban government encourages and supports sports programs. These programs begin in the primary schools, where outstanding young athletes are singled out and channeled toward ever-higher levels of competition. These programs have recently proved their worth as Cuba's athletes have begun competing successfully in the Olympics and other international competitions. Sports activities are not restricted to schools; many trade unions and neighborhood groups also sponsor teams.

Baseball remains the number-one sport in Cuba. From junior leagues to international competitions, the game attracts people of all ages and abilities. Cubans follow the progress of the North American major leagues almost as closely as they follow their own teams. Other popular sports include boxing, sailing, gymnastics, basketball, swimming, golf, tennis, track and field, and jai alai, a game resembling handball that originated in Spain.

Currency

The unit of money in Cuba is the *peso*. The peso is divided into 100 units called *centavos*. At current exchange rates, one US dollar is worth 76 Cuban centavos. Cuban paper money has colorful pictures of José Martí and other figures from the revolution for independence from Spain.

Tourists in Cuba are generally required to make purchases with money from their own countries. This helps the government acquire "hard currency." This is money from the United States and Europe that can be used to buy needed imports. Cuba needs this money because the country generally does business with the Soviet Union, which trades items rather than exchanges money.

Cuban currency in the form of two twenty-peso notes and a one-peso coin.

Language

Spanish is the official language of Cuba. Because of the influence of the United States between 1898 and 1959, many older adults also speak English. Today, schools and universities stress the study of foreign languages — especially Russian and English.

Havana

Havana, Cuba's capital city, has a population of over 2 million people — almost 20% of the country's total population. Founded in 1515, Havana is one of the oldest and most picturesque cities in the Western Hemisphere. Its museums, parks, cultural attractions, and beaches have made it one of the more popular tourist spots in the Caribbean. Besides being the seat of the government and main tourist attraction, the city also serves as the country's main industrial, educational, and commercial center.

Havana's charm comes from its blend of the old and the new. The city's colonial section, Habana Vieja, or Old Havana, contains many places of historical interest. Buildings erected by the Spanish stand beside modern high-rise buildings and brand-new parks and recreational centers. A United Nations grant is currently funding the restoration of many of Old Havana's narrow cobblestone streets and its colonial landmarks. The United Nations has designated Old Havana as one of the most important remaining historical sites in Latin America.

Cubans in North America

After the Cuban revolution of 1959, 500,000 people left Cuba and settled in Spain, the United States, and other countries in Latin America. Most of these people were from the middle or upper classes, but some lower-income Cubans also left the country. Many of them had sided with the Batista dictatorship in the guerrilla war of 1956-59 and felt compelled to leave. Today, over one million Cuban-Americans live in Canada and the United States. Many Cubans living in the United States reside in Florida.

Glossary of Useful Cuban (Spanish) Terms

barco (BAR-coh) .... boat
calle (KAH-yeh) .... street
castillo (cas-TEE-yoh) .... castle

conquistadores
    (kohn-kees-tuh-DOOR-rays) ...."conquerers"; Spanish colonists
escuela (es-KWAY-lah) ....school
esgrima (es-GREE-mah).......................the sport of fencing
helado (ay-LAH-doh) ....ice cream
malecón (mah-leh-KOHN)...................seawall or dike
mundo (MOON-doe) ....world
pañuelo (pah-NWEH-loh)....................bandanna or handkerchief
playa (PLAH-yah) ....beach
primaria (pree-MAH-ree-ah) ....grade school (elementary)
punta (POON-tah)...............................point of land, peninsula
secundaria (seh-koon-DAH-ree-uh).......junior or senior high school

More Books about Cuba

Here are some more books about Cuba. If you are interested in them, check your library. They may be useful in doing research for the "Things to Do" projects.

Cuba. Vázquez and Casas (Childrens Press)
Cuba from Columbus to Castro. Williams and McSweeney (Julian Messner)
Cuba in Pictures. Lerner Publications Department of Geography Staff (Lerner)
From Mexico, Cuba, and Puerto Rico. Garver and McGuire (Dell)

Things to Do — Research Projects

As Fidel Castro came to power, he had the support of most Cubans, who had been struggling beneath a corrupt government. The people believed that Castro sought the kind of government that they did. But since that time, over a million Cubans have left their homeland, dissatisfied with Castro's leadership or discouraged by economic conditions resulting, in part, from restrictive US trade policies. As you read about Cuba and its political scene, you will want current facts. Some of the research projects and activities that follow need accurate, up-to-date information. Two publications that your library may have will tell you about recent newspaper and magazine articles on many topics:

Readers' Guide to Periodical Literature
Children's Magazine Guide

For accurate answers to questions about Cuba, look up *Cuba* in these two publications. They will lead you to recent articles.

1. Fidel Castro came to power with the favor of both the Cuban people and other people throughout the world. Since then, he has lost much of this

support. Find out more about Castro, why he has lost and gained favor with Cubans in particular periods in the past, and how people in Cuba feel about him today.

2. Cuba's location in the Caribbean has been both an advantage and a disadvantage throughout its history. Find out more about Cuba and its location. What advantages and disadvantages does its position bring?

More Things to Do — Activities

These projects are designed to encourage you to think more about Cuba. They offer ideas for projects that you can do at home or at school.

1. As Alain saw at the poster exhibit, Cuba's billboards and posters make statements about current Cuban and world concerns. See if you can find examples of these political posters and sketch them.

2. Draw a map of Cuba showing its position in the world. Plot Havana, the Bay of Pigs, the Isle of Youth, and the Caribbean Sea on the map. Can you see the island's crocodile shape?

3. Alain was surprised to learn that many North Americans eat only one ice-cream cone at a time. Learn more about any of Cuba's customs that surprised you.

4. If you would like to have a Cuban pen pal, write to these people:

International Pen Friends
P.O. Box 290065
Brooklyn, NY 11229

Worldwide Pen Friends
P.O. Box 39097
Downey, CA 90241

Be sure to tell them what country you want your pen pal to be from. Also include your full name, age, and address.

Perched atop the seawall known as the Malecón, Alain waves good-bye.

Index